# NOVAK DJ

## Biography

The Life of a Serbian Tennis
Player as the greatest legend in the
Game

## Steve Clowers

This book is a non-fiction work founded on the author's research and experiences. While every effort has been exerted to ensure the precision and comprehensiveness of the information provided, neither the author nor the publisher assumes responsibility for any errors, omissions, or damages resulting from the utilization of the information contained herein.

# Content

# Introduction

Novak Djokovic, a big name in tennis, comes from Belgrade, Serbia. He faced tough times growing up in war-torn Yugoslavia. He started playing tennis when he was young and quickly became really good. In 2008, he won a big tournament called the Australian Open, marking the beginning of an amazing career full of victories and hard work.

Djokovic isn't just known for winning matches; he's part of a famous rivalry with other top players like Roger Federer and Rafael Nadal.

Together, they've made tennis more exciting with intense matches and memorable moments.

But Djokovic's impact goes beyond the tennis court. He's also involved in charity work, has businesses, and believes in taking care of his overall well-being. His ability to stay strong in tough situations on the court shows not just his skills but also his determination and strength.

When you learn about Novak Djokovic, you discover a story that's more than just scores and games. It's about overcoming challenges, working hard, and reaching for greatness.

# *Chapter 1*

.

## The Early Life of the Legend

Born on May 22, 1987, in Belgrade, Serbia, Novak Djokovic is renowned as one of tennis's greatest players. His early life was shaped by a family deeply immersed in tennis, running a pizzeria in Belgrade. Djokovic's interest in tennis began at a young age, starting his training at four under his father, Srdjan. Despite facing the challenges of wartime

Yugoslavia in the 1990s, Djokovic remained committed to tennis.

In 2003, Djokovic turned professional at 16, making a notable impact the following year by reaching Wimbledon's third round. Known for his agility, potent backhand, and unmatched work ethic, Djokovic's breakthrough occurred in 2007 when he secured his first Grand Slam title at the Australian Open. Throughout his early career, he engaged in fierce rivalries with tennis legends like Federer and Nadal, showcasing mental fortitude and an unwavering pursuit of excellence.

His accomplishments include holding all four Grand Slam titles concurrently in 2015-2016. Djokovic's journey from a challenging childhood in Belgrade to tennis greatness reflects not only his skill but also his resilient and determined mindset. His narrative stands as a testament to his extraordinary talent and unwavering commitment to the sport.

# Chapter 2

## Rise through the Ranks

Novak Djokovic's ascent in professional tennis is a captivating story marked by skill, tenacity, and an unwavering pursuit of greatness. Over more than two decades, he transformed from a promising young talent into a dominant force, achieving numerous milestones, Grand Slam victories, and a remarkable climb to the world No. 1 ranking.

Embarking on his professional journey in 2003, Djokovic swiftly garnered attention for his exceptional abilities. Progressing steadily through the rankings, he displayed a playing style characterized by precision, agility, and a potent baseline game. The turning point arrived in 2007 when he secured his inaugural Grand Slam title at the Australian Open, defeating Jo-Wilfried Tsonga in the final. This triumph marked the initiation of Djokovic's rise to the upper echelons of men's tennis.

As he honed his skills, Djokovic faced formidable adversaries in Roger

Federer and Rafael Nadal, sparking intense rivalries that defined a tennis era. His duels with these legends, particularly in Grand Slam finals, underscored his mental fortitude and ability to thrive under pressure.

The pivotal year of 2011 showcased Djokovic at his peak. A remarkable 41-match winning streak, including victories over Federer and Nadal, saw him clinch three Grand Slam titles – the Australian Open, Wimbledon, and the US Open – firmly establishing his dominance. Djokovic's consistency, physical fitness, and adaptability across various surfaces propelled him to new heights.

Adaptability has been a cornerstone of Djokovic's success, excelling on hard courts, clay, and grass alike. This versatility has been a significant factor in his sustained success and longevity in a sport demanding excellence across diverse playing conditions.

The pursuit of the career Grand Slam became a central theme in Djokovic's narrative. Achieving this rare feat in 2015-2016, he became the first man since Rod Laver in 1969 to hold all four Grand Slam titles simultaneously. This historic accomplishment solidified his status as one of tennis's all-time greats.

While Djokovic's on-court achievements are extraordinary, his mental resilience and dedication to improvement have been equally vital to his ascent. Overcoming setbacks, injuries, and adversity, Djokovic's commitment to physical fitness and mental conditioning sets a benchmark for aspiring tennis players.

The "Big Three" rivalry, featuring Djokovic, Federer, and Nadal, has been a central narrative in men's tennis for over a decade. Djokovic's rise to the top of this elite group symbolizes an era of unprecedented competition and excellence, pushing the boundaries of what's achievable in tennis.

Djokovic's consistency in maintaining an elite level of play over the years is remarkable. Winning Grand Slam titles in multiple years and holding the world No. 1 ranking exemplify his ability to compete at the highest level. His enduring greatness, despite challenges from the younger generation, cements his status as one of tennis's true legends.

Beyond the court, Djokovic's contributions extend to sportsmanship, philanthropy, and global tennis promotion. His impact transcends tennis, making him a revered figure in the sports world.

Novak Djokovic's climb through the ranks is a saga of extraordinary skill, unwavering determination, and a pursuit of excellence. From a promising talent in Belgrade to a tennis legend, Djokovic's journey has left an indelible mark on the sport. His ability to navigate challenges, overcome adversity, and consistently deliver outstanding performances establishes him as an icon of tennis, with his influence shaping the sport's future for years to come.

# Chapter 3

## Dominance and World No. 1 Ranking

Novak Djokovic's extraordinary dominance in men's tennis unfolds as a captivating narrative of exceptional skill, unwavering determination, and an unrelenting pursuit of excellence. This overarching journey not only encompasses the establishment and continuous retention of the World No. 1 ranking but also features a multitude of record-breaking accomplishments, Grand Slam victories, and historic winning streaks. Djokovic's ascent to the zenith of tennis greatness is a story of sustained brilliance, shaped by his meticulous approach, mental resilience, and a remarkable ability to redefine the benchmarks of success in the sport.

The pivotal juncture in Djokovic's climb to the World No. 1 ranking unfolded in 2011, marking the culmination of years of dedication and consistent performances on the ATP Tour. In that remarkable year, Djokovic embarked on a season of unprecedented success, securing three out of the four Grand Slam titles—the Australian Open, Wimbledon, and the US Open. This extraordinary feat not only inscribed his name in tennis history but also propelled him to the apex of the rankings, displacing the long-standing No. 1, Rafael Nadal.

What ensued was an era of unparalleled dominance that would come to define Djokovic's illustrious career. His extraordinary consistency, adaptability to various playing surfaces, and ability to perform at the pinnacle in crucial moments firmly established him as the unequivocal leader of men's tennis. Djokovic's reign wasn't merely a statistical achievement; it was a manifestation of his unparalleled skills, mental resilience, and an enduring commitment to excellence.

At the core of Djokovic's supremacy was his record-breaking success in maintaining the World No. 1 position. Week after week, he continued to occupy the top spot, surpassing records set by his legendary counterparts, Roger Federer and Rafael Nadal. Djokovic's capacity to sustain this position over extended periods showcased not only his on-court prowess but also his mental fortitude and longevity in a sport renowned for its physical and mental demands.

Grand Slam triumphs emerged as a defining feature of Djokovic's dominance. His consistent ability to reach the latter stages of major tournaments and secure Grand Slam titles underscored his era as one of tennis's greatest. Djokovic's meticulous preparation, strategic acumen, and exceptional physical fitness were pivotal to his success on the grandest stages in tennis.

The years 2015-2016 witnessed Djokovic achieve a historic milestone, further solidifying his place among tennis immortals. He became the first man since Rod Laver in 1969 to concurrently hold all four Grand Slam titles. This extraordinary feat, often dubbed the "Nole Slam" or "Djoker Slam," highlighted his versatility and dominance across different surfaces. Djokovic's ability to conquer each major championship in rapid succession not only etched his name in the record books but also established him as a player for the ages.

Historic winning streaks further underscored Djokovic's unparalleled dominance. In 2011, he embarked on a staggering 41-match winning streak, a feat that showcased his ability to consistently outclass opponents. This streak, which included victories over his main rivals, Roger Federer and Rafael Nadal, added an extra layer of significance to his achievements. Djokovic's ability to maintain such high levels of play over an extended period was a testament to his physical fitness, mental resilience, and sheer skill.

Beyond the statistics and records, Djokovic's dominance is characterized by his mental toughness and his ability to handle pressure. His capacity to turn the tide in matches, especially when facing adversity, has been a defining trait throughout his career. Djokovic's performances in decisive moments, often in Grand Slam finals, have solidified his reputation as a player who not only excels under pressure but thrives on it.

The narrative of Djokovic's dominance extends beyond the tennis court, encapsulating his impact on the sport and the global tennis community. His relentless pursuit of excellence, sportsmanship, and dedication to continuous improvement have set a benchmark for aspiring players. Djokovic's influence reaches beyond individual accomplishments, embodying a commitment to the highest standards of professionalism and athletic achievement.

In conclusion, Novak Djokovic's dominance in men's tennis, particularly in establishing and maintaining the World No. 1 ranking, is a saga of extraordinary success. His record-breaking accomplishments, Grand Slam triumphs, and historic winning streaks paint a comprehensive picture of a player who has not only left an indelible mark on the sport but has redefined the standards of success in tennis. Djokovic's ability to sustain excellence over an extended period, adapt to different challenges, and consistently deliver outstanding performances cements his legacy as one of the greatest players to have graced the courts. As he continues to etch his name in the record books, Djokovic's impact on the sport and its future remains profound.

# Chapter 4

## Competitive Showdowns and Unforgettable Matches

Novak Djokovic's tennis journey is distinguished not only by his individual achievements but also by the intense rivalries and unforgettable matches that have characterized his era. These rivalries, particularly with icons like Roger Federer and Rafael Nadal, underscore Djokovic's prowess on the court and significantly contribute to the rich tapestry of men's tennis history. Among these remarkable encounters, the Wimbledon 2018 final stands out as a prime example of Djokovic's resilience and his ability to shine under pressure.

The establishment of rivalries with tennis icons has been a defining element of Djokovic's career. The "Big Three" era, featuring Djokovic, Federer, and Nadal, has been a central narrative in men's tennis for over a decade. Each player brings a unique style and personality to the court, enhancing the global appeal of the sport. Djokovic's battles against Federer and Nadal have been particularly enthralling, showcasing the highest levels of skill, determination, and sportsmanship.

Facing Roger Federer, Djokovic has participated in some of the most memorable and closely contested matches in tennis history. Their rivalry goes beyond mere statistics, with each encounter carrying the weight of anticipation and excitement. The 2019 Wimbledon final, lasting nearly five hours, is a standout moment. Djokovic emerged victorious in a fifth-set tiebreaker, securing his fifth Wimbledon title and 16th Grand Slam overall. The level of play, drama, and sheer determination displayed by both players turned this match into an instant classic.

The rivalry with Rafael Nadal has added another layer of intensity to men's tennis. Djokovic and Nadal have faced each other in numerous Grand Slam encounters, each match a spectacle of endurance and skill. The Australian Open 2012 final is particularly memorable, as Djokovic outlasted Nadal in an epic five-set battle lasting nearly six hours. This match not only attested to Djokovic's physical and mental toughness but also highlighted the rivalry's capacity to produce tennis of the highest order.

The trio's rivalries extend beyond Grand Slam finals, permeating various tournaments and surfaces. Djokovic's ability to consistently compete at the highest level against two of the sport's greatest players underscores his status as one of the era's defining figures. These rivalries have not only captivated tennis enthusiasts but have elevated the sport to new heights, with each player pushing the boundaries of what is achievable on the court.

Iconic matches against other contenders have also played a significant role in shaping Djokovic's legacy. Encounters with Andy Murray, Stan Wawrinka, and Juan Martin del Potro have added additional layers of competition and drama to the tennis landscape. The 2012 Australian Open final against Murray, where Djokovic triumphed in a marathon five-setter, showcased his ability to withstand relentless pressure and emerge victorious in crucial moments.

Facing Stan Wawrinka, particularly in Grand Slam tournaments, Djokovic encountered a formidable opponent who tested his physical and mental resilience. The 2015 French Open final stands out, where Wawrinka denied Djokovic the elusive Roland Garros title in a hard-fought four-set battle. Despite the defeat, Djokovic's ability to rebound from setbacks and continue pushing the boundaries of his game became evident in the subsequent years.

The 2016 Rio Olympics witnessed Djokovic facing Juan Martin del Potro in a memorable first-round match. In a contest that lasted over four hours, Djokovic succumbed to Del Potro, highlighting the unpredictable nature of tennis and the formidable challenges posed by opponents outside the "Big Three." While the loss was a disappointment for Djokovic, it showcased the depth of talent in men's tennis and the unpredictable nature of the sport.

One of the most unforgettable matches in Djokovic's career occurred at Wimbledon in 2018. The epic final against Kevin Anderson lasted over five hours and featured grueling rallies, incredible shot-making, and a display of mental fortitude from both players. Djokovic ultimately emerged victorious in straight sets, securing his fourth Wimbledon title. This match showcased Djokovic's ability to thrive in the most challenging circumstances and his unwavering focus during critical moments.

The Wimbledon 2018 final against Anderson encapsulated Djokovic's resilience, strategic prowess, and physical endurance. After overcoming an elbow injury that had impacted his form in 2017, Djokovic's return to the pinnacle of the sport was solidified with this Wimbledon triumph. The match was not only a display of Djokovic's exceptional tennis skills but also a testament to his mental toughness as he navigated the pressure of a Grand Slam final with unparalleled composure.

Throughout his career, Djokovic's ability to forge rivalries and engage in memorable matches has been a key factor in his legacy. These encounters have not only showcased his skills on the court but have also contributed to the evolution of men's tennis. Djokovic's rivalry with Federer and Nadal, in particular, has elevated the sport to new heights, creating a narrative that transcends individual accomplishments and adds layers of drama and excitement to tennis tournaments worldwide.

In conclusion, Novak Djokovic's career is intricately woven with intense rivalries and memorable matches against tennis icons and formidable contenders alike. His battles with Federer and Nadal, as well as other notable opponents, have defined an era of men's tennis marked by unprecedented competition and excellence. Each match, whether in Grand Slam finals or other tournaments, contributes to the rich tapestry of Djokovic's legacy, showcasing his skill, resilience, and ability to deliver under pressure. The Wimbledon 2018 final, in particular, stands as a crowning moment in Djokovic's career, symbolizing his triumphant return to the summit of men's tennis. As Djokovic continues to add chapters to his storied career, the anticipation and excitement surrounding his rivalries and matches remain a central aspect of the tennis landscape.

# Chapter 5

## Off-Court Pursuits and Personal Life

Novak Djokovic is more than just a tennis superstar - his impact goes beyond the court, revealing a diverse individual whose influence reaches far beyond the world of sports. Apart from his incredible achievements in tennis, Djokovic actively engages in philanthropy and ventures into various businesses. His family life, including marriage and fatherhood, adds a personal touch to his public image. However, Djokovic's off-court journey is not without its share of challenges and controversies, shedding light on the complexities that come with global fame.

Djokovic's dedication to making a positive impact is evident through the Novak Djokovic Foundation, founded in 2007. The foundation focuses on early childhood education in Serbia, aiming to give children access to quality preschool programs. Djokovic believes in the transformative power of early learning, and his foundation reflects this commitment.

Beyond tennis, Djokovic has also delved into the business world. He has founded several companies, including "Family Sport," managing his brand and diverse business interests. This business side of Djokovic showcases his strategic thinking and his desire to leave a legacy beyond his accomplishments in tennis.

**Family Life: Marriage, Children, and Personal Milestones**

Away from the spotlight, Djokovic's personal life is filled with significant moments. His marriage to Jelena Ristic in 2014 marked a joyful celebration of commitment. Jelena has been a constant pillar of support throughout Djokovic's career, and their relationship, which began in the early 2000s, has grown into a strong partnership.

The Djokovic family expanded with the arrival of their son, Stefan, in 2014, and their daughter, Tara, in 2017. Djokovic often shares glimpses of his family life on social media, providing fans with a more intimate view. Balancing the demands of professional tennis with family life highlights Djokovic's ability to navigate the complexities of a global sports career while maintaining strong connections with loved ones.

Personal milestones, such as Djokovic embracing fatherhood and marriage, add depth to his public image, showcasing a well-rounded individual who values life beyond the tennis court. His dedication to family life emphasizes the importance he places on maintaining a grounded and fulfilling personal life amidst the challenges of a high-profile career.

## Challenges and Controversies Off the Court

While Djokovic has enjoyed immense success on the tennis court, his off-court journey has had its share of challenges and controversies. One notable incident was in 2020 when Djokovic organized the Adria Tour, aimed at fundraising for humanitarian causes. Unfortunately, the events faced criticism for not adhering to COVID-19 safety protocols, resulting in several players, including Djokovic, testing positive for the virus.

The Adria Tour controversy highlighted the responsibilities that come with being a global sports figure, especially during a pandemic. Djokovic, acknowledging the missteps, expressed regret and used the experience for reflection and growth.

Another source of controversy has been Djokovic's stance on vaccination. His vocal hesitancy to receive the COVID-19 vaccine, citing personal beliefs and concerns, has sparked discussions about the role of athletes in promoting public health measures and the responsibility they bear as public figures.

In addition to these controversies, Djokovic has faced challenges in balancing his personal views with the expectations of being a global ambassador for tennis. Navigating the delicate balance between expressing personal beliefs and upholding the image of a sports icon highlights the complexities athletes face at the intersection of sports and societal issues.

Despite these challenges, Djokovic's off-court journey reflects resilience and a commitment to personal growth. Controversies have provided opportunities for reflection and learning, emphasizing that even the most accomplished athletes are continually evolving individuals dealing with the complexities of the human experience.

Novak Djokovic's off-court pursuits and personal life offer insight into the multi-faceted individual behind the tennis legend. His philanthropic initiatives and business ventures showcase a commitment to making a positive impact beyond the sports arena. Djokovic's family life, with its milestones and challenges, adds depth to his public persona, illustrating the intricacies of balancing a high-profile career with personal relationships. The controversies and challenges he has faced off the court provide a nuanced perspective on the responsibilities and expectations placed upon global sports figures. Djokovic's journey beyond tennis is a narrative of growth, resilience, and an ongoing quest for a meaningful and impactful life beyond the confines of the tennis court.

# Chapter 6

## Mind and Body: The Djokovic Approach

Novak Djokovic's journey to the pinnacle of professional tennis isn't solely due to his physical prowess; it's a result of a holistic approach that intertwines mental resilience, physical fitness, and a commitment to overall well-being. The Djokovic Approach, as it's coined, transcends traditional sports training, embodying a philosophy that acknowledges the interconnectedness of mind and body.

## Foundations of Djokovic's Mental Game

At the core of Djokovic's unparalleled success lies his mental resilience and unwavering mindset. His ability to navigate high-pressure situations, rebound from setbacks, and stay focused during critical moments goes beyond sheer mental strength. Collaborating with sports psychologists, Djokovic employs techniques like visualization, mindfulness, and meditation to craft a mindset that extends beyond individual matches and contributes to the consistency of his career.

Djokovic's mental fortitude isn't confined to the court; it's a crucial aspect of handling the demands and scrutiny of professional tennis off the court. This ability to maintain a positive mindset in the face of challenges underscores a holistic understanding of mental well-being that complements his on-court performances.

## *Physical Fitness and Nutrition of the Legend*

Djokovic's physical prowess is a result of a year-round commitment to peak athletic performance. His agility, speed, and endurance on the court are products of a rigorous training regimen that blends on-court exercises with gym sessions, cardiovascular workouts, and agility drills.

The Djokovic Regimen extends beyond traditional physical training to include a meticulous focus on nutrition. Djokovic's gluten-free and predominantly plant-based diet isn't a mere dietary trend but a strategic decision rooted in its positive impact on his energy levels and overall well-being. Collaborating with nutritionists, Djokovic tailors his diet to meet the specific demands of his training and tournament schedule, emphasizing the symbiotic relationship between a well-maintained body and mental resilience.

## Elevating Beyond the Court

What sets the Djokovic Approach apart is its holistic understanding of health and well-being that goes beyond conventional athletic training. Djokovic's commitment to holistic well-being is evident in his exploration of alternative therapies and practices that contribute to his overall health.

The incorporation of sensory deprivation tanks for relaxation and mental rejuvenation is one notable facet of Djokovic's holistic approach. These flotation tanks provide a weightless experience, promoting deep relaxation and mental clarity. Djokovic's embrace of alternative therapies reflects an openness to methods that complement traditional training.

Alongside alternative therapies, Djokovic includes yoga and Pilates in his routine, enhancing flexibility, core strength, and balance—essential components for a tennis player's agility. This holistic approach emphasizes a harmonious balance between physical, mental, and emotional well-being.

Djokovic's commitment to well-being extends beyond personal health to advocacy for sustainability and environmental consciousness. His involvement in eco-friendly initiatives showcases a broader commitment that aligns with his overall philosophy of balance and interconnectedness.

## The Djokovic Approach: A Holistic Philosophy

In essence, the Djokovic Approach is a comprehensive philosophy that views the mind and body as interconnected facets of overall well-being. Djokovic's journey isn't just about winning matches; it's a testament to the symbiotic relationship between mental resilience, physical fitness, and a holistic approach to health.

The Djokovic Approach isn't a set of isolated training techniques; it's a way of life reflecting Djokovic's profound understanding of the intricate interplay between mind and body. As Djokovic continues to shape his career, this approach serves as a testament to the power of a holistic approach in achieving sustained success in sports and beyond. It's a blueprint that aspiring athletes and enthusiasts alike can draw inspiration from—a philosophy transcending tennis, offering insights into the broader realm of human potential.

# Chapter 7

## The Grand Slam Chase

Novak Djokovic's tennis legacy is intricately woven into his relentless pursuit of Grand Slam excellence. This journey unfolds through his aspirations for the Calendar Year Grand Slam, his monumental achievements at each major leading to the Career Grand Slam, and the historic milestone of securing and surpassing 20 Grand Slam titles, a feat that cements his name in the history of tennis.

## Chasing the Calendar Year Grand Slam: A Quest for Immortality

The Calendar Year Grand Slam, a rare and prestigious accomplishment, involves winning all four major championships in a single calendar year. Djokovic's pursuit of this elusive feat has been marked by near misses and tantalizingly close encounters with tennis immortality.

In 2011, Djokovic embarked on a phenomenal season, clinching three Grand Slam titles consecutively.

However, his quest for the Calendar Year Grand Slam was halted by Roger Federer in the semifinals of the French Open. Although falling short that year, Djokovic's dominance signaled a shift in tennis dynamics.

The prospect of the Calendar Year Grand Slam emerged again in 2015. Djokovic secured the Australian Open, the US Open, and Wimbledon, leaving the French Open as the final hurdle. Once again, the red clay of Roland Garros proved challenging, with Djokovic stumbling in the final against Stan Wawrinka. The dream slipped away, but Djokovic's resilience and consistency across surfaces became defining aspects of his game.

In 2021, Djokovic found himself on the cusp of history at the US Open after triumphing at the Australian Open and Wimbledon earlier in the year. Despite a valiant effort in a dramatic final against Daniil Medvedev, the pursuit of the Calendar Year Grand Slam was thwarted. Djokovic's quest remained unfulfilled, adding complexity to his Grand Slam narrative.

## Novak's Triumphs Across the Majors

While the Calendar Year Grand Slam remained a tantalizing goal, Djokovic achieved the Career Grand Slam—a monumental milestone in its own right. The Career Grand Slam entails winning each of the four major championships over the course of a player's career. Djokovic's journey toward this accomplishment reflects his adaptability across different surfaces and his ability to conquer diverse challenges.

Djokovic secured his first major title at the 2008 Australian Open, signaling the beginning of a remarkable career. However, it wasn't until 2011 that he claimed his second major at Wimbledon. The subsequent years witnessed a surge in Djokovic's dominance, with victories at the US Open (2011, 2015) and the Australian Open (2012, 2013, 2015, 2016) forming the foundation of his Career Grand Slam.

The final piece of the puzzle fell into place in 2016 at Roland Garros. Djokovic, renowned for his mastery on hard courts, conquered the challenging clay of the French Open, defeating Andy Murray in the final. The Career Grand Slam was now a reality, and Djokovic joined the esteemed ranks of tennis legends who had achieved this rare feat.

## 20 Grand Slam Titles: Equaling and Surpassing Records

As Djokovic etched his name into the tennis history books with the Career Grand Slam, his pursuit of Grand Slam supremacy continued. The milestone of 20 Grand Slam titles became the next significant target, and Djokovic approached this achievement with unwavering determination.

The journey to the 20th title was marked by historic moments. Djokovic equaled the record for most Grand Slam titles by a male player with his victory at the 2021 French Open, securing his 19th major. This set the stage for a historic bid to equal and eventually surpass his greatest rivals, Roger Federer and Rafael Nadal.

Wimbledon 2021 witnessed Djokovic's record-tying moment. In a captivating final against Matteo Berrettini, Djokovic showcased his trademark resilience and skill. With the iconic Centre Court as the backdrop, Djokovic clinched his 20th Grand Slam title, standing shoulder to shoulder with Federer and Nadal at the pinnacle of men's tennis.

Surpassing the 20-title mark marked Djokovic's ascent to the summit of men's tennis. His ability to consistently perform at the highest level across all surfaces and against various opponents showcased a level of excellence that places him among the greatest to have ever played the sport.

As Djokovic continues his Grand Slam journey, the narrative is far from its conclusion. The pursuit of the Calendar Year Grand Slam, the Career Grand Slam, and the relentless quest for additional Grand Slam titles form an ongoing saga. Djokovic's place in tennis history is secure, and his impact extends beyond mere numbers and records.

The Grand Slam Pursuit encapsulates the challenges, triumphs, and the unwavering commitment of Novak Djokovic to leave an enduring mark on the sport. Whether the Calendar Year Grand Slam becomes a reality or the tally of Grand Slam titles continues to rise, Djokovic's journey is a testament to his resilience, adaptability, and his enduring quest for tennis greatness. The Grand Slam Pursuit is a saga that unfolds with every swing of Djokovic's racquet, leaving tennis enthusiasts worldwide in anticipation of the next captivating chapter in this extraordinary tennis odyssey.

# Chapter 8

## Facing Challenges and Bouncing Back

Novak Djokovic's road to tennis stardom isn't a smooth ride—it's a story marked by ups and downs, with setbacks and inspiring comebacks at its core. From dealing with injuries that tested his physical strength to navigating the controversies of the 2021 US Open, Djokovic's ability to overcome tough times stands out as a key part of his incredible career.

## *Dealing with Injuries: Overcoming Physical Hurdles*

Playing professional tennis takes a toll on even the best athletes, and Djokovic is no exception. His career has seen its fair share of injuries that really put his physical well-being to the test. These challenges turned out to be moments of growth for Djokovic, showcasing not only his physical resilience but also his mental strength.

One tough period happened in 2017 when Djokovic struggled with an elbow injury. This led to a drop in his performance, early exits in tournaments, and a decline in his world ranking. But Djokovic didn't let this get him down. Instead, he took a break from the sport to address his physical issues and refresh his mental approach.

His time away turned out to be crucial. Djokovic came back stronger, winning the Wimbledon title in 2018. This victory wasn't just a return to form but also a testament to Djokovic's resilience in the face of physical challenges.

However, the journey back to the top had its twists. The 2020 US Open presented a unique set of challenges. Djokovic, returning after a break due to the global pandemic, faced disqualification in the fourth round for accidentally hitting a line judge with a ball. It was a setback, but Djokovic's response showed his ability to confront adversity.

## 2021 US Open: Controversies and Rising Again

The 2021 US Open was a showcase of Djokovic's knack for dealing with controversies and making impressive comebacks. With his eyes set on the Calendar Year Grand Slam, Djokovic was the favorite entering the tournament. However, the road to making history wasn't an easy one.

In the final against Daniil Medvedev, Djokovic faced a tough opponent and a loud New York crowd. The pressure was intense, and controversies over vaccine mandates and Djokovic's vaccination status added more challenges.

Despite the off-court distractions, Djokovic's on-court performance was brilliant. The final turned into a tennis spectacle, with both players giving their all. Djokovic, despite his best efforts, fell short against Medvedev's inspired play. The dream of the Calendar Year Grand Slam remained unfulfilled.

The defeat was bitter, but Djokovic's reaction showed his resilience. He showed sportsmanship, acknowledging his opponent's triumph and the difficulties he faced. Djokovic's ability to bounce back from both on-court defeat and off-court distractions highlighted his mental strength and his capacity to turn setbacks into stepping stones.

# The Comeback Recipe of Djokovic

Novak Djokovic's comebacks go beyond the tennis court; they reflect a mental strength honed through adversity. His ability to overcome injuries, deal with controversies, and rise above setbacks reveals a mindset that thrives in challenging situations.

For Djokovic, a comeback starts with a careful approach to healing and physical conditioning. Working with his team of experts, he tailors training plans that address specific weaknesses and ensure a gradual return to peak fitness. This commitment to the physical aspect of his game is complemented by a steadfast focus on mental well-being.

Mental resilience is at the heart of Djokovic's comebacks. His ability to stay calm under pressure, handle setbacks, and maintain unwavering self-belief sets him apart. Djokovic often talks about using visualization and mindfulness in preparing for matches, techniques that contribute to his mental toughness.

Experience plays a crucial role in Djokovic's comebacks. Every setback becomes a chance to learn, a moment to adjust strategies, and an opportunity for self-improvement. Djokovic's enduring success at the top of the tennis world reflects his ability to evolve and adapt, turning setbacks into platforms for growth.

## The Djokovic Resilience Quotient

Novak Djokovic's ability to bounce back from challenges and setbacks can be described as the "Djokovic Resilience Quotient." This means he's really good at overcoming tough times and staying strong, not just in tennis but also when dealing with fame, media attention, and off-court distractions. Whether it's facing controversies or handling pressure, Djokovic's resilience shows that he can handle difficult situations and still keep going. It's like a measure of how well he can come back stronger after facing tough moments.

The Djokovic Resilience Quotient shines through in his response to controversies, such as the vaccination debates and the incident at the 2020 US Open. Djokovic's ability to weather storms, stay focused amidst external noise, and emerge with his competitive spirit intact showcases a resilience that goes beyond the tennis court.

In the grand story of Djokovic's career, setbacks aren't roadblocks but integral chapters that contribute to the narrative of his legacy. The ability to face challenges head-on, learn from them, and come back stronger defines Djokovic's lasting impact on the sport.

As Novak Djokovic continues his tennis journey, the story of setbacks and comebacks remains an open book. The rhythm of victories and defeats, the ups and downs of physical challenges and mental triumphs, weave a tale that goes beyond just numbers and records.

Djokovic's career is a reminder that champions aren't defined by the absence of challenges but by their ability to overcome them. Each setback becomes a setup for a great comeback, each defeat a platform for future victories. The Djokovic saga, with all its complexities and nuances, reminds us that the true measure of an athlete's greatness lies not just in their victories but in their ability to endure and emerge stronger from the crucible of setbacks. The story continues, and with every chapter, Djokovic adds new dimensions to the melody of his enduring legacy.

# Chapter 9

## A Legacy That Goes Beyond Tennis

Novak Djokovic isn't just a tennis legend; his impact reaches far beyond the court. Let's delve into how he's reshaped the game, his charitable efforts, and why he's become a global sporting icon.

### Changing the Game of Tennis

Djokovic's influence on tennis is more than just winning titles. His unique playing style, blending athleticism, mental strength, and all-court mastery, has transformed the sport. Initially known for his defensive skills, Djokovic evolved into a complete player, dominating from the baseline and excelling at the net.

His mental resilience shines in critical moments, turning the tide in his favor. Think of the 2019 Wimbledon final where he faced championship points against Roger Federer and not only saved them but went on to win the match. Such moments underscore Djokovic's mental tenacity and his ability to thrive under pressure.

In the era of the "Big Three," Djokovic's rivalries with Federer and Nadal have elevated tennis to new heights. His battles, especially the "Fedalovic" clashes, are etched in tennis history.

## Making a Difference Beyond Tennis

Djokovic's impact isn't confined to the court; he's making a difference in the world through philanthropy.

The Novak Djokovic Foundation, established in 2007, focuses on providing underprivileged children in Serbia with quality education. The "School of Life" program, part of the foundation, aims to enhance preschool education by creating stimulating learning environments.

During the COVID-19 pandemic, Djokovic initiated the Adria Tour to raise funds for relief efforts. Despite facing criticism, his intent to contribute to the fight against the pandemic was clear. Djokovic and his wife, Jelena, also donated one million euros to support hospitals in Serbia.

Beyond health crises, Djokovic has shown environmental consciousness. He pledged donations to support the restoration of fire-ravaged areas in Australia, showcasing his awareness of global environmental challenges.

## *Internationally Recognized Sports Icon*

Djokovic's influence extends globally, turning him into a sporting icon. His journey from war-torn Serbia to tennis stardom inspires aspiring athletes worldwide. Djokovic has become a cultural bridge, fostering national pride in Serbia and the Balkan region. His success resonates as a source of collective pride.

Advocating for player welfare, Djokovic played a crucial role in establishing the Professional Tennis Players Association (PTPA) in 2020. While it sparked debates, his involvement reflects a commitment to addressing systemic issues in tennis governance.

Novak Djokovic's legacy is a living story of resilience, compassion, and a commitment to making a positive impact. On the court, he's rewritten the rules of tennis. Off the court, his philanthropy and advocacy redefine what it means to be a global sporting icon.

As Djokovic continues to navigate fame, competition, and social impact, his legacy unfolds dynamically. It's a story of inspiration for the next generation, a force for positive change, and a testament to the transformative power of sports. In the grand tapestry of sporting legacies, Novak Djokovic has woven a narrative that resonates with fans, aspiring athletes, and advocates for positive change worldwide.

## Influence on Young Football Stars

Novak Djokovic's impact reaches beyond the tennis court, inspiring young footballers around the world. His journey from challenging circumstances to global sports stardom serves as a powerful source of motivation for aspiring football players.

Djokovic's resilience, hard work, and mental strength are qualities that resonate across different sports, including football. Young footballers can find inspiration in his ability to overcome obstacles, both in his sports career and personal life. Djokovic's commitment to constant improvement, adaptability, and a never-ending pursuit of greatness offers valuable lessons for those aiming to succeed in the competitive realm of sports.

Moreover, Djokovic's dedication to making a positive impact through philanthropy, especially with the Novak Djokovic Foundation, sets a compelling example. It emphasizes the broader responsibilities that come with success in sports. Young footballers can learn not only from Djokovic's athletic achievements but also from his commitment to contributing to the well-being of communities.

In essence, Novak Djokovic's influence on young footballers goes beyond just playing the game. It encompasses a mindset of resilience, a passion for continuous improvement, and an understanding of the positive impact athletes can have beyond the field. Djokovic's story serves as a motivating force for the next generation of footballers who aspire to leave their mark on the sport and the world.

# The Conclusion

As we reach the final chapters of Novak Djokovic's life story, it's like stepping back and taking in the incredible journey of a true champion—a journey that goes beyond the tennis court. Djokovic's life unfolds like a captivating symphony, filled with moments of triumph, challenges that tested his spirit, and an unbreakable will to succeed.

From growing up in war-torn Serbia to becoming a global tennis icon,

Djokovic's story is not just about winning titles; it's about overcoming the tough times life threw at him. The Grand Slam victories, his historic No. 1 rankings, and those unforgettable matches against Federer and Nadal paint a picture of a player who didn't just play tennis; he redefined it.

But, like any great story, Djokovic's journey had its share of obstacles—injuries, controversies, and the dream of achieving the Calendar Year Grand Slam. Instead of diminishing his brilliance, these challenges showcased his incredible resilience, becoming a source of inspiration for athletes everywhere.

As we wrap up this biography, it's clear that Djokovic's symphony is far from over. Each turn of the page hints at more to come—on the court and beyond.

On the court, we can look forward to Djokovic pursuing even greater heights and facing off against the next generation of talented players. The quest for the Calendar Year Grand Slam remains an unfulfilled ambition, offering him a chance to etch his name even deeper into tennis history.

Off the court, Djokovic's journey extends into philanthropy and advocacy. The Novak Djokovic Foundation, with its focus on education and making a positive impact, is set to create new stories of change. Djokovic's role in advocating for player welfare, as seen in the establishment of the Professional Tennis Players Association (PTPA), shows his commitment to a fairer tennis environment.

So, as we close this chapter, it's not an ending but a pause—a chance to reflect on what's been and a sense of excitement for what's yet to unfold. Djokovic's remarkable career is like a symphony in progress—an unfinished masterpiece that keeps us eagerly waiting for the next beautiful note. The tennis court is his stage, and each match adds a new melody to the legacy he continues to build.

In this reflection, we find not just a list of achievements but a living story—a tale of resilience, inspiration, and an everlasting pursuit of greatness. Djokovic's legacy is a symphony that continues to play on, echoing through the history of tennis and touching the hearts of fans, aspiring athletes, and admirers all around the world.

# Definition of Terms

**Dynamic Serbian Player:**

Novak Djokovic, born on May 22, 1987, in Belgrade, Yugoslavia, stands out as a remarkable Serbian tennis professional.

**Grand Slam Maestro** Djokovic's illustrious career boasts an impressive tally of 20 Grand Slam singles titles, marking him as a true titan in the tennis world.

**Early Tennis Journey**

Initiating his tennis journey at four and turning professional in 2003,

Djokovic exhibited promise from a young age.

## Junior Triumphs

Noteworthy achievements in his junior career include clinching the Australian Open boys' singles title in 2004.

## World's Top-Ranked Player

Djokovic ascended to the world No. 1 ranking in 2011, maintaining this prestigious position for extended durations.

## Mastery of Hard Court Play

His playing style shines on hard courts, where Djokovic has carved out a legacy of success.

## Part of the Big Three Rivalry

Djokovic actively contributes to the legendary tennis rivalry alongside Roger Federer and Rafael Nadal, collectively known as the "Big Three."

## Ambassador for Serbian Tennis

Djokovic has played a pivotal role in elevating the global status of Serbian tennis.

## Physical Conditioning Excellence

Known for unparalleled fitness, Djokovic's rigorous training routine contributes significantly to his on-court endurance.

**Mental Fortitude**

One of his defining attributes is his mental resilience, often orchestrating comebacks in challenging match situations.

**Australian Open Dominance**

Djokovic boasts a remarkable track record at the Australian Open, securing multiple titles Down Under.

**Completion of Career Grand Slam**

Achieving a Career Grand Slam, Djokovic has triumphed in each of the four major tournaments at least once.

**Davis Cup Contributions** Djokovic's contributions have been instrumental in Serbia's victorious Davis Cup campaigns.

## Family's Supportive Role

His family has played a crucial role in his tennis journey, offering unwavering support throughout.

## Philanthropic Involvement

Djokovic actively engages in philanthropy, supporting causes such as children's healthcare and education.

**Memorable 2012**

The year 2012 marked a milestone as Djokovic became the fifth player to win three Grand Slam titles in a single calendar year.

**Record-Setting**      **Achievements**

Djokovic holds numerous records, including the longest ATP World Tour No. 1 ranking streak.

**Olympic Aspirations:**

Despite challenges, Djokovic expresses a strong desire to secure an Olympic gold medal for Serbia.

**Key Coaching Partnership** The collaboration with coach Marian Vajda has been pivotal in shaping Djokovic's career trajectory.

**Iconic Tennis Rivalries** Djokovic's fierce on-court battles with Federer and Nadal have etched unforgettable moments in tennis history.

**Breakthrough in 2008:**
Global attention turned to Djokovic in 2008 when he clinched his first Grand Slam title at the Australian Open.

**Mediterranean Influence**

Djokovic's upbringing in the Mediterranean region is evident in both his playing style and demeanor.

**Strategic Serve and Return Skills**

His playing style is characterized by strategic serve and return prowess, crucial components of his game.

**Global Tennis Ambassador**

Djokovic serves as a global ambassador for tennis, actively promoting the sport on the international stage.

Cultural Impact: His success has elevated the status of tennis in

Serbia and the broader Balkan region.

**Endorsement by Adidas:** Djokovic maintains enduring partnerships with major brands, including Adidas.

**Diversified Professional Portfolio**

Beyond tennis, Djokovic is involved in various business ventures, adding diversity to his professional pursuits.

**Emphasis on Nutritional Discipline:** Recognized for his strict diet, Djokovic underscores the importance of nutrition in athletic performance.

## 2020 U.S. Open Controversy

Djokovic faced disqualification at the 2020 U.S. Open for accidentally hitting a line judge.

## Fan Connection

Djokovic maintains a strong connection with fans worldwide, often engaging with them on social media.

## Versatile Imitations

Known for mimicking other players' styles, Djokovic showcases his versatility on the court.

## Navigating COVID-19 Challenges

Djokovic encountered challenges related to COVID-19 protocols during the 2020 tennis season.

## Advocate for Fair Play

Despite on-court intensity, Djokovic is an advocate for fair play and sportsmanship.

## Earnings through Record Prize Money:

His on-court success translates into substantial prize money earnings.

## Founder of Tennis Academy

Djokovic established the Novak Djokovic Tennis Academy, nurturing young tennis talents.

**Masters Titles Streak:**

He boasts an impressive collection of ATP Masters 1000 titles, highlighting his consistent excellence.

**Tiebreak Mastery:**

Djokovic's proficiency in tiebreaks often proves decisive in closely contested matches.

**2021 Calendar Grand Slam Pursuit**

Djokovic made a historic attempt at a Calendar Grand Slam in 2021.

**Triumphs at Roland Garros**

Winning at Roland Garros completed his Career Grand Slam and solidified his tennis legacy.

### Endurance in Physically Intense Matches

Djokovic's fitness is tested in matches known for their physical intensity and prolonged duration.

### UNICEF Ambassador Role

He serves as a UNICEF Goodwill Ambassador, actively contributing to children's welfare.

**Adaptable Playing Style** Djokovic's adaptability on different surfaces showcases his versatility as a player.

**Media Focus** His achievements are often accompanied by media scrutiny and heightened public attention.

**Balancing Act as a Tennis Parent:** Djokovic became a father in 2014, managing the delicate balance between family life and his demanding tennis career.

**Celebratory On-Court Rituals** His on-court celebrations, such as the sliding splits, add a touch of entertainment to his matches.

**Athlete's Mindset:**

Djokovic's mindset as a professional athlete emphasizes continuous improvement and growth.

**Australian Open Marathon Matches:**
He participated in some of the longest Grand Slam matches in history at the Australian Open.

**Tech-Savvy Training Approach**
Djokovic incorporates technological advancements in his training and preparation.

**2022 Season Highlights:** Djokovic's performances in the 2022 season continued to showcase his tennis prowess.

**Evolutionary Legacy:** As Djokovic continues his tennis journey, his legacy as one of the sport's greatest players continues to evolve.

Printed in Great Britain
by Amazon